Book Two
Early Intermediate

A DOZEN A DAY
SONGBOOK

PLAYBACK+
Speed • Pitch • Balance • Loop

Each piece includes two audio tracks: one with piano and orchestration at a practice tempo,
and one with just the orchestration at a faster performance tempo. With our exclusive
Playback+ feature, you can change the tempo even more without altering the pitch,
plus set loop points for continuous repetition of tricky measures.

To access audio, visit:
www.halleonard.com/mylibrary

"Enter Code"
1050-3318-3161-6473

ISBN 978-1-4803-4211-8

EXCLUSIVELY DISTRIBUTED BY

WILLIS MUSIC

HAL•LEONARD®
7777 W. BLUEMOUND RD. P.O. BOX 13819
MILWAUKEE, WISCONSIN 53213

Visit Hal Leonard Online at
www.halleonard.com

NOTE TO TEACHERS

This collection of Broadway, movie and pop hits can be used on its own or as supplementary material to the iconic *A Dozen A Day* technique series by Edna Mae Burnam. The pieces have been arranged to progress gradually, applying concepts and patterns from Burnam's technical exercises whenever possible. Teacher accompaniments and suggested guidelines for use with the original series are also provided.

These arrangements are excellent supplements for any method and may also be used for sight-reading practice for more advanced students.

CONTENTS

4   This Land Is Your Land

6   Hallelujah

8   Moon River

10   I Dreamed a Dream

13   A Whole New World

16   I Want to Hold Your Hand

18   Once Upon a Dream

20   You Raise Me Up

23   I Walk the Line

26   In the Mood

4

This Land Is Your Land

Use with A Dozen A Day Book 2,
after Group I (page 12).

Words and Music by
Woody Guthrie
Arranged by Carolyn Miller

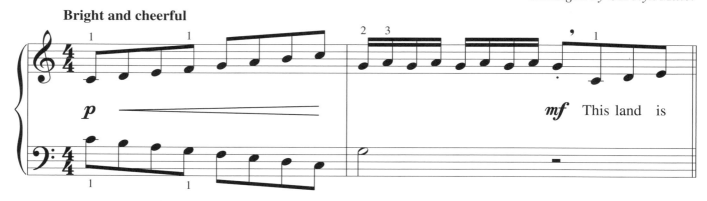

this land was built for you and me.

Hallelujah

Use after Group I (page 12).

Words and Music by
Leonard Cohen
Arranged by Carolyn Miller

Moderately, with growing intensity

Moon River
from the Paramount Picture BREAKFAST AT TIFFANY'S

Use after Group II (page 18).

Words by Johnny Mercer
Music by Henry Mancini
Arranged by Carolyn Miller

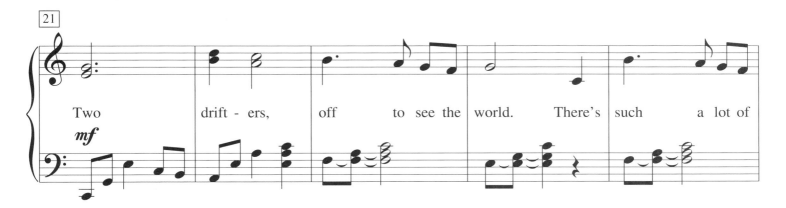

Two drift - ers, off to see the world. There's such a lot of

mf

world to see. _____ We're af - ter the same

cresc.

rain - bow's end, _____ wait- in' 'round the bend, my Huck - le - ber - ry friend,

f

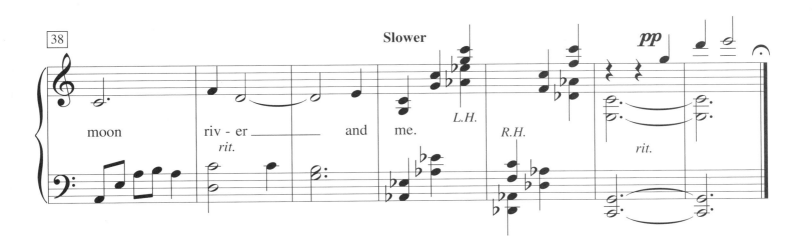

moon riv - er _____ and me.

rit.

Slower

L.H. *R.H.*

pp

rit.

I Dreamed a Dream
from LES MISÉRABLES

Use after Group II (page 18).

Music by Claude-Michel Schönberg
Lyrics by Alain Boublil, Jean-Marc Natel
and Herbert Kretzmer
Arranged by Carolyn Miller

Andante cantabile

With pedal

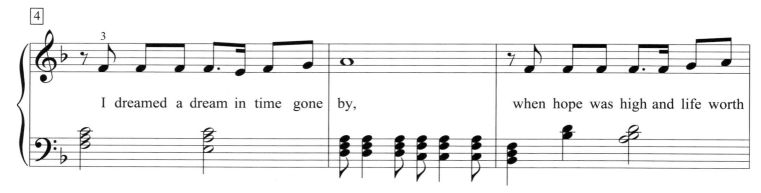

I dreamed a dream in time gone by, when hope was high and life worth

liv- ing. I dreamed that love would nev- er die.

I dreamed that God would be for- giv- ing. Then I was young and un- a-

fraid, and dreams were made and used and wast - ed.

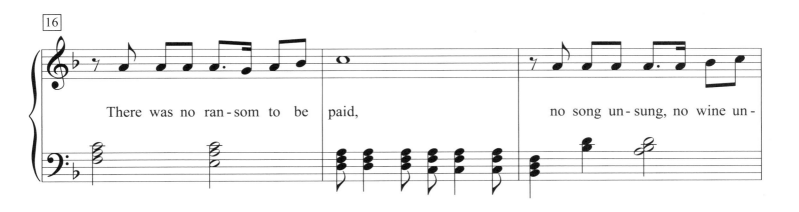

There was no ran - som to be paid, no song un - sung, no wine un -

tast - ed. But the ti - gers come at night

with their voic - es soft as thun - der, as they tear your hope a -

part,   as they turn your dream to   shame.

A Whole New World

from Walt Disney's ALADDIN

Use after Group III (page 25).

Words by Alan Menken
Lyrics by Tim Rice
Arranged by Carolyn Miller

2019/19

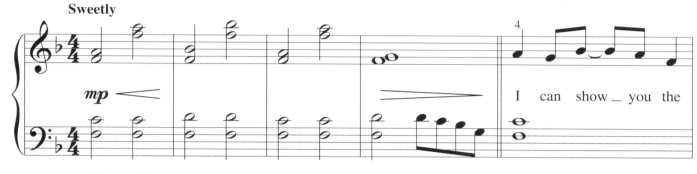

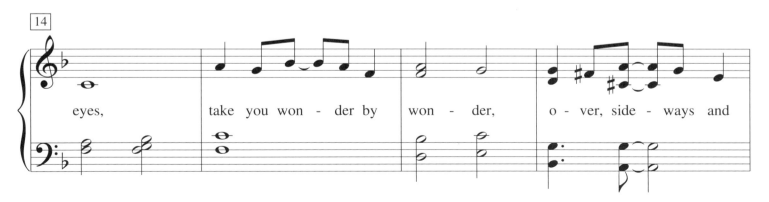

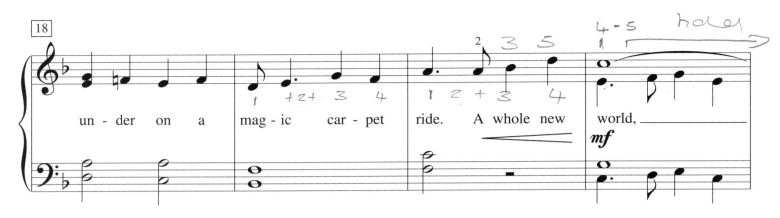

un-der on a mag-ic car-pet ride. A whole new world,_____

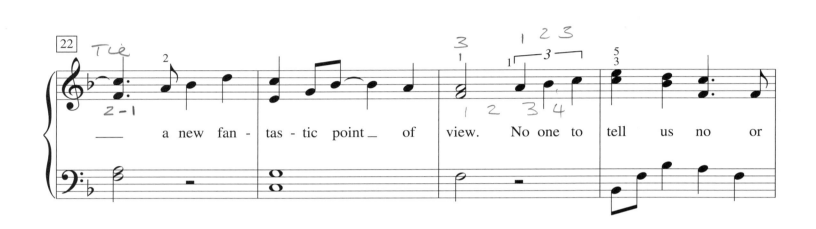

_____ a new fan-tas-tic point__ of view. No one to tell us no or

where to go or say we're on-ly dream-ing. A whole new world,_____

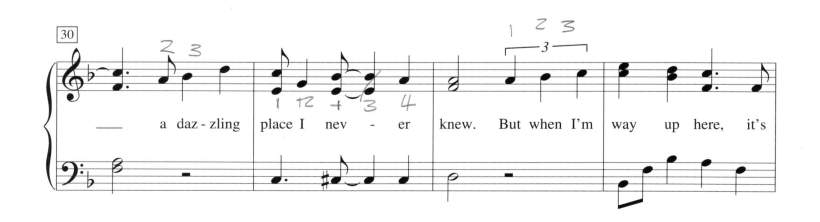

_____ a daz-zling place I nev - er knew. But when I'm way up here, it's

crys - tal clear that now I'm in a whole new world with you. _____

_____ A whole new world, *L.H.* that's where we'll be. *L.H.*

A thrill - ing chase, a won - drous place for you and me.
rit.   *a tempo*

rit. *p*

I Want to Hold Your Hand

Use after Group III (page 25).

Words and Music by John Lennon
and Paul McCartney
Arranged by Carolyn Miller

Once Upon a Dream
from Walt Disney's SLEEPING BEAUTY

Use after Group IV (page 31).

Words and Music by Sammy Fain
and Jack Lawrence
Adapted from a theme by Tchaikovsky
Arranged by Carolyn Miller

You Raise Me Up

Use after Group IV (page 31).

Words and Music by Brendan Graham
and Rolf Lovland
Arranged by Carolyn Miller

22

I Walk the Line

Use after Group V (page 38).

Words and Music by
John R. Cash
Arranged by Carolyn Miller

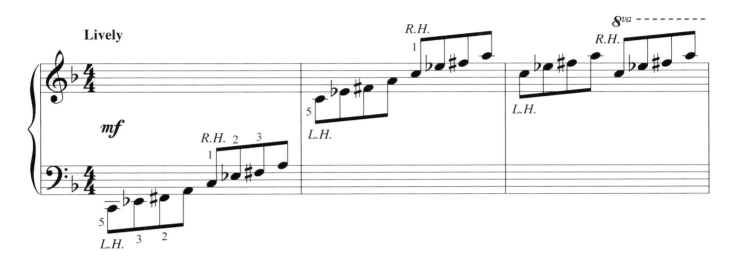

I keep a close watch on this heart of mine.

Yes, I'll ad - mit that I'm a fool for you.

Be - cause you're mine, I walk the line.

In the Mood

Use after Group V (page 38).

By Joe Garland
Arranged by Carolyn Miller

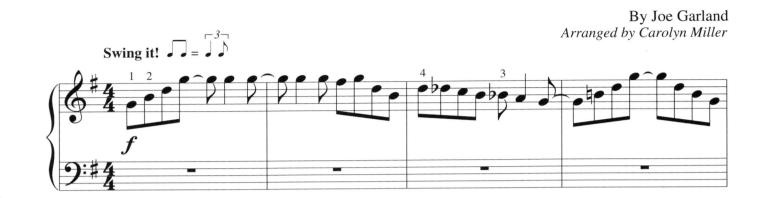

28

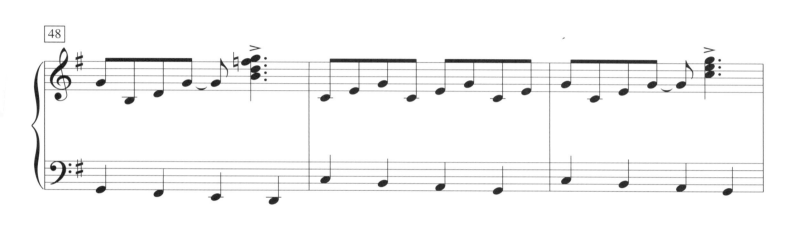

A DOZEN A DAY SONGBOOK SERIES

BROADWAY, MOVIE AND POP HITS

Arranged by Carolyn Miller

The *A Dozen a Day Songbook* series contains wonderful Broadway, movie and pop hits that may be used as companion pieces to the memorable technique exercises in the *A Dozen a Day* series. They are also suitable as supplements for ANY method!

MINI
EARLY ELEMENTARY
Songs in the Mini Book:
Any Dream Will Do • Can You Feel the Love Tonight • A Dream Is a Wish Your Heart Makes • Heigh-Ho • I'm Popeye the Sailor Man • It's a Grand Night for Singing • Lean on Me • Love Me Tender • So Long, Farewell • You'll Never Walk Alone.

00416858 Book Only $7.99

00416861 Book/Audio $12.99

PREPARATORY
MID-ELEMENTARY
Songs in the Preparatory Book:
The Bare Necessities • Do-Re-Mi • Getting to Know You • Heart and Soul • Little April Shower • Part of Your World • The Surrey with the Fringe on Top • Swinging on a Star • The Way You Look Tonight • Yellow Submarine.

00416859 Book Only $7.99

00416862 Book/Audio $12.99

BOOK 1
LATER ELEMENTARY
Songs in Book 1:
Cabaret • Climb Ev'ry Mountain • Give a Little Whistle • If I Were a Rich Man • Let It Be • Rock Around the Clock • Twist and Shout • The Wonderful Thing About Tiggers • Yo Ho (A Pirate's Life for Me) • Zip-A-Dee-Doo-Dah.

00416860 Book Only $7.99

00416863 Book/Audio $12.99

BOOK 2
EARLY INTERMEDIATE
Songs in Book 2:
Hallelujah • I Dreamed A Dream • I Walk the Line • I Want to Hold Your Hand • In the Mood • Moon River • Once Upon A Dream • This Land is Your Land • A Whole New World • You Raise Me Up.

00119241 Book Only $6.99

00119242 Book/Audio.............. $12.99

Prices, content, and availability subject to change without notice.

WILLIS MUSIC

EXCLUSIVELY DISTRIBUTED BY

Hal•Leonard®

www.willispianomusic.com   www.facebook.com/willispianomusic

0716

A DOZEN A DAY

by *Edna Mae Burnam*

The **A Dozen A Day** books are universally recognized as one of the most remarkable technique series on the market for all ages! Each book in this series contains short warm-up exercises to be played at the beginning of each practice session, providing excellent day-to-day training for the student. All book/audio versions include orchestrated accompaniments by Ric Ianonne.

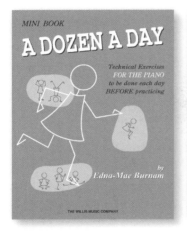

MINI BOOK
00404073 Book Only $5.99
00406472 Book/Audio $9.99

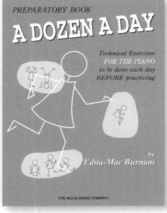

PREPARATORY BOOK
00414222 Book Only $5.99
00406476 Book/Audio $9.99

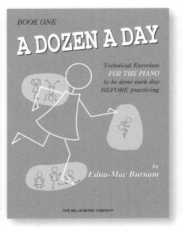

BOOK 1
00413366 Book Only $5.99
00406481 Book/Audio $9.99

BOOK 2
00413826 Book Only $5.99
00406485 Book/Audio $9.99

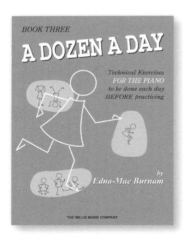

BOOK 3
00414136 Book Only $6.99
00416760 Book/Audio $10.99

BOOK 4
00415686 Book Only $6.99
00416761 Book/Audio $10.99

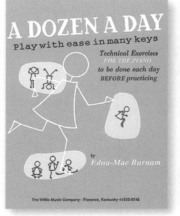

PLAY WITH EASE IN MANY KEYS
00416395 Book Only $5.99

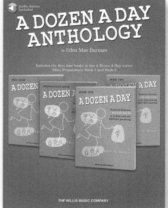

A DOZEN A DAY ANTHOLOGY
00158307 Book/Audio $24.99

ALSO AVAILABLE:
The **A Dozen A Day Songbook** series containing Broadway, movie, and pop hits!

Visit Hal Leonard Online at **www.halleonard.com**

WILLIS MUSIC

EXCLUSIVELY DISTRIBUTED BY

HAL•LEONARD®

Prices, contents, and availability subject to change without notice. Prices listed in U.S. funds.

0716